MUKEDI DIESTA - MPUTU Delphin

Writing a scientific paper in Business Informatics

MUKEDI DIESTA - MPUTU Delphin

Writing a scientific paper in Business Informatics

ScienciaScripts

Cover image: www.ingimage.com

This book is a translation from the original published under ISBN 978-620-6-71046-2.

Publisher:
Sciencia Scripts
is a trademark of
Dodo Books Indian Ocean Ltd. and OmniScriptum S.R.L publishing group

120 High Road, East Finchley, London, N2 9ED, United Kingdom
Str. Armeneasca 28/1, office 1, Chisinau MD-2012, Republic of Moldova, Europe
Printed at: see last page
ISBN: 978-620-8-13786-1

Prelude

Scientific works in general, and in business informatics in particular, are of great importance because the authors normally have to deal with subjects that are topical in relation to the period/year in which they are written.

Our professional experience has led us through all these twists and turns to date, and so we are leaving these writings available to all scientists (without exception), even though computer science is covered here.

Unfortunately! Current promotions sometimes do the opposite of what is expected of them. And why is that?

During this interrogation, at least eight key assertions were made, all of which were of concern:

1- The wrong basis from the previous curriculum, which the learner only studies out of complacency;
2- Incompetence due to this bad start;
3- Disability due to a number of distractions, especially the wave of android phones/social networks;
4- The wrong choice of course and supervisor;
5- Lack of study time or failure to revise subjects regularly at home;

6- The problem where the learner is distracted and doesn't know where to start and where to finish?

7- Sometimes they even lack the appropriate tools to guide them, despite the knowledge they have acquired.

8- Lack of listening (abstinence from advice) Etc.

Let's just say that a handful of them give their all to this task.

The big difficulty is knowing what kind of people we are training for tomorrow's future.

Let's not cross our arms, we framers and educators, let's stand up forever, contributing in one way or another; so that this exceptional wrist can defend itself and replace us tomorrow.

The purpose of this manual is to remedy the situation in which :

- How and where to start a scientific project ;
- The different stages of scientific work ;
- The choice of framer ;
- Data collection ;
- Drafting responsibilities ;
- The actual writing of a scientific paper.

It appeals to computer scientists but, out of intellectual curiosity, there is advice for all scientists.

We urge all supervisors and learners to be aware of what you do and what you are, because tomorrow you will be alone on the field of application, at which point your intellectual proclivity will be naked, if there is no proof, then what a disgrace!

On the other hand, if you're gifted enough to have an exceptional wrist, hats off to you.

Let's get away from bad collaborators, let's work for our exclusive future; because the gain has always been individual, not even for the supervisors, not even for the parents and others; given that the decision to share the spoils is made by oneself (the interested party).

Courage, let's make the most of our skills, because in them we'll be able to eat and drink freely, as Bernard Dadier says in one of his books: "Work ensures independence".

"The author

Introduction

Most of today's scientific work has lost its value in terms of form and content. This is due to a number of factors for which responsibility is shared:

- the learners themselves;
- the framers ;
- tutors and the State

We're not going to go into everything here, but it should be noted that these responsibilities to be shared are, of course, first and foremost the responsibility of the learner, because at this level of Higher and University Education, we're dealing with mature people who already have the virtue of good and evil, even though they've been trained: "andragogy".

So this workshop shows them just how much they themselves are responsible for their future in terms of the choice of framer, subject and acquisition of materials.

In this context, tutors and the State are partners who must support and advise you on your career path.

We emphasise that, as learners, you are committed to becoming useful in society tomorrow, when it will be your turn to lead. To do this, acquiring knowledge has a great influence because it will make you tall and lead you to great heights.

All the different efforts you make together will contribute to your well-being in tomorrow's future. Make the most of it, by avoiding evasions on all fronts, i.e. anything that could contribute to your failure or incompetence.

In this manual, you'll find a few tips for growing up.

The world belongs to the brave and the vigilant, they say.

Scientific work reflects the value of its author in terms of his or her skills and scientific knowledge, although plagiarism is rife as a result of poor choice of supervisor and increased incompetence. Nonetheless, any scientific discipline urges us to refer to the work of others and not to copy and paste, with no reason to exist in the subject being explored.

Change, change for your well-being, for your know-how, society needs you.

GENERAL POINTS ABOUT WRITING A SCIENTIFIC PAPER.

We want to guide our readers by at least clarifying the basic concepts of our title: "La ***Rédaction d'un Travail Scientifique surtout en informatique de gestion en République Démocratique du Congo***".

When you produce a scientific paper, you need to know what it is intended to achieve and what its objective is, both in general and in business informatics in particular.

Besides, is this book just for computer scientists?

To this concern, let's say yes on the one hand, no on the other, how?

No, for the simple reason that any researcher who learns about it will have gained at least one useful element that contributes in one way or another to his or her knowledge.

Yes, specifically for IT specialists, because they are responsible for the content from start to finish.

In the Democratic Republic of Congo, because the pragmatic experience comes from there.

Despite this, science being universal, we dare to believe that all the guidelines set out in this book are universal, and even IT institutions elsewhere will have at least some points in common.

Let us at least understand that a researcher/scientist is any man of science who displays his know-how in a field of his choice, to the detriment of others.

And the essay, which is a dissertation on a subject that the author makes available to others to expose what has eaten away at his intellect so that readers can benefit from it.

If the wording is understood in this way, work, from the Latin: trepalium, instrument of torture, but torture, not in the sense of harming the human body, torture, in the sense of perpetual occupation, adding that it is :

- human activity, applied to production, creation and maintenance; the effort required to do something.
- Also, a task (activity) that gives him life, what makes him live.
- all research undertaken in a field of knowledge.

Science, from the Latin: "scienta, de scire, savoir", is a coherent body of knowledge relating to certain categories of facts, objects or phenomena that obey laws and are verified by experimental methods:

- Human sciences, focusing on man and his behaviour,
- Exact sciences, using calculations and

experimentation.

Scientific: that which relates to science; scientific research, which is in the field of knowledge, has the characteristics of rigour and the demand for objectivity that are characteristic of the sciences.

Generally speaking, scientific work is a body of research rigorously backed up by precise methods, specific to a particular field and with a very well-defined purpose.

This book focuses on how to write a scientific paper: final year/cycle paper, dissertation, thesis, internship report.

These are scientific exercises that meet the rigorous standards of computer science so that they express their primary objective.

Computer science is an exact science, which advocates the strict application of its principles to achieve the desired result.

Cycle I and Cycle II researchers in particular will find the outline of their work in the illustration.

It is a compulsory test for all finalists in the 1er cycle or 2ème cycle, according to the Ministry of Higher and University Education in the Democratic Republic of Congo, and has a threefold objective:

1- Meet the Ministry's requirements;

2- A test demonstrating the knowledge acquired since previous studies up to the level of this first cycle; oriented in a precise field, an expression of what, the author is capable in this acquisition of knowledge,

3- An endorsement of his competence and quality as a university executive worthy of his name to defend his commitment to serving others.

In business informatics, this is an opportunity for them to demonstrate how they have designed their software, which runs in the blink of an eye, especially the key element they are looking for. This is for the graduate cycle.

Whereas in the second cycle, whatever the direction, the engineer must be able to present an IT project resulting from his knowledge of design to implementation with an overall cost ranging from :

- Number and estimated cost of personnel to be credited for this project;
- Materials to be adapted, quantity and quality specifying the cost too;
- Time, duration of execution, in order to accumulate all these global costs as stated above.

1- Emergence of terms

Two useful words, and we want to understand them well:

1- Work: (from Latin (trepalium, instrument of torture),

- human activity applied to the production, creation or maintenance of something.
- activity deployed to complete a task[1] .

2- Scientific (science): (from Latin scire, to know)

- a body of knowledge relating to certain categories of facts; objects or phenomena that obey laws and are verified by experimental methods .

2- The difference between intellectual work and scientific work.

1- **Intellectual work**[2] , it comes from the mind, from the spirit, originating in the knowledge or rational knowledge acquired, for a given result of understanding. It must meet standards.

- it is a process of the intellect by which it constructs ideas, the action of reflecting, of examining an idea or a situation through thought.
- noun phrase, a form of activity that produces written documents.

e.g.: - administrative work (service assignment report)

- a speech,
- minutes,
- a newspaper,
- a magazine,
- an article,

[1] Le petit Larousse illustré, 2009 p 1029
[2] www.languefrançaise.uliege.be

- an interview,
- a letter
- etc.

2- Scientific work is based on scientific knowledge,

1- General considerations on scientific knowledge.[3]

We acquire scientific knowledge by several means, in particular: by personal experience every day, by the experience of others, by good follow-up, reflection . .and also in schools in the field of knowledge for good quality.

This involves researching, selecting and using valid and identifiable resources linked to works/authors.

It can be understood in terms of its content, i.e. as a producer of scientific and technical knowledge and information.

The various current interpretations of the terms information and knowledge lead us to clarify the definitions used here.

2- Characteristics of scientific work

All scientific knowledge must have :

- The Objective,
- Abstraction (summary)
- The introduction

[3] Infotrack.unige

- Methods and techniques
- the results
- The discussion
- The conclusion

References

When we talk about the objective, we are talking about a fact that needs to be grasped, described and produced many times over.

E.g.: Socio-economic fact, social fact.

Scientific knowledge must be precise and accurate, communicable and explainable.

For a good assessment, it must be well oriented so that its communication and explanations are explicit and the expected results can be seen.

2- Stage of a scientific project

The steps involved in scientific work are :

a- The title of the topic to be discussed or developed.

At this level, the theme must be well chosen to demonstrate what needs to be amplified so that the operators understand the reflex or the appropriate object which is the driving force behind all the copy.

This may be the expression of the problem, requiring resolution whose course is all along the symptomatic lines.

b- Hypotheses (formulation)

They are constructive voices of research while

groping for answers to the problem posed in the formulation of the theme.

c- The operational phase (conducting an experiment). This phase consists of amplifying the pragmatic ideas of the subject, going from one point to another proving the pros and cons.

d- Law enforcement (application of the principles of the domain) or data recovery

e- Interpreting the data

This interpretation of the data is tantamount to saying that the object that has revolutionised the author must be well specified by using the lived reality and dressing it up in the subject or field in which he specialises.

f- Concluding and publishing articles

A summary should enliven readers after they have gone through the whole book.

g- Sharing the results with the scientific community, which is what the author communicates in his book, teaching others what you know from others. And they will have found it worthwhile to have gone through it instead of having wasted their time.

h- Repeat the experiment (if necessary), a scientific work as outlined above, can be its own experiment or that of others or an innovation, this will demonstrate how it will join the others work in its field.

This is where we have to live the particularity of each scientific or technical field, by putting these laws, principles of verification: axioms and postulates so that the field declares itself concrete and precise.

Science cannot go beyond its own criteria; it embodies them and praises them, and respects them unfailingly.

According to the dictionary, principles are the basic notions of a science or discipline. For philosophers,[4] principle comes from the Latin principium, "beginning", a concept of primary truths or propositions that serve to demonstrate other truths, but cannot themselves be demonstrated, by virtue of their primary character and simplicity.

According to: le Petit Larousse illustré 2009, principles are propositions accepted as the basis of reasoning, generally theoretical rules that guide and lead to general laws governing a set of phenomena, verified by the accuracy of the consequences: knowledge, elementary rules of a science.

Principles are like the first elements of human knowledge, and play the same role in relation to it as axioms do in mathematics. Aristotle retained at least two principles, the principle of contradiction (it is

[4] Diesta-Mputu Delphin, Questions Approfondies d'Informatique de Gestion (QAIG), L1 Informatique, unpublished 2024

impossible for a thing to be and simultaneously not to be) and the principle of the third-excluded (a thing is true or false, but there is no middle term - a "third" - between the contradictories).

Not all principles are the same, so they are strains, sources with particular characteristics that fiercely support this discipline with a view to certifying in its own right what it is and what it is worth.

If Aristotle, the philosopher, is talking about contradiction, let's talk about respecting principles and not respecting them. Respecting principles means achieving the objectives set by the discipline, because it advocates respect, whereas not respecting principles means misapplying them, which leads to failure.

All scientific work is intellectual, but not all intellectual work is scientific.

Scientific work is based on a precise, well-directed framework, requiring laboratory experiments, which must make use of universal values relating to verifiable facts and absolutely appropriate methods and techniques. Observations, experiments, hypotheses and deductions:

- Natural sciences,
- Human sciences,
- Exact/pure sciences,

- Education (life) sciences,
- Ect.

By way of illustration, our scientific work includes :

- End-of-cycle (end-of-studies) work,
- Memory
- Thesis
- Internship report,
- Scientific work (scientific book, literary work).

The value of a scientific or intellectual work :

- He is the author, the conspirator, the embodiment of what he is and what he is worth, which is why we insist on respect for the appropriate principles.

For the author, the quality assurance value[5] advocated by the philosopher Jean Onaothso in his book "L'assurance qualité et le système LMD à l'Université Catholique du Congo" (Quality assurance and the LMD system at the Catholic University of the Congo) is a culture of excellence in which several partners must be involved to achieve a good result. But as we have said, the author/learner is the very first person responsible for making a total commitment to his or her training, quality and know-how, before anyone else.

[5] Jean Onaothso K., L'assurance qualité et le système LMD à l'Université Catholique du Congo, p145

The mediocrity that is rampant in today's society, in which some people sift is worthwhile, and defends itself unfailingly.

This is our concern so that every author, researcher and learner shines like a star, given that :

- The work is the mirror exposing what it is and who the author is. It expresses the value and that of the author in relation to standards: theme, content, form and field of exploitation.
  - Expression is the clarification of the ideas expressed, so the expression must be simple, clear and comprehensible if the content is to be of benefit to everyone.
- The author: must demonstrate his knowledge, which he shares with others:
  - Objective
  - Order
  - Useful, i.e. of interest to the

    masses/readers
  - Adding value to the world of science
  - Contribute in one way or another to the archiving process.
  - A good background

- A good theme
- And in good shape.

Let's just say that between a scientific work and an intellectual work a nuance blurs most people, but is it that the clarification starting from the different ideas expressed here are worth discerning well.

As pointed out above, all scientific work is intellectual, but not all intellectual work is scientific. While referring to the arguments put forward and demonstrated.

From the illustrations, a letter or a report cannot compare with or equal a mathematics or physics book.

We understand that when Fauchier wrote the physics book or when Robert Reix wrote the computer science book, they did not all have the same orientation as Seder Senghor and Fontaine when they wrote the French texts.

CHAPTER 1: WRITING A SCIENTIFIC PAPER ON BUSINESS COMPUTING

1- Choice of subject

Candidates are free to choose their subject, taking into account :

- assurance of data delivery ;
- the skills to get by;
- understanding of the subject ;
- the field of investigation/ environment

If we are talking about free choice, in relation to the author himself, because the aim is to achieve the objective and the choice does not become an obstacle so that the end is not reached.

Sometimes certain subjects are disproved in the field, so to avoid all this, judicious thought needs to be given to them from the outset.

2- Formulating the subject

If we refer to the course of scientific research, each field has its own particularities that must ipso facto be respected, a subject can be treated in a different way and relative to its field, so that each draws valid consequences sanctioning the expected result.

As for IT, in the first cycle as the interested party has to produce software in the formulation of the subject a reflection of the implementation and realization must be expressed or still felt, it will additionally have to live the IT terms in it. For example:

1-Computerisation of the management of stocks of out-of-date pharmaceutical products: the case of Prima Pharma
2-Setting up and implementing a database for calculating hillsides in a university institution: the case of the Institut Supérieur de Développement Rural (ISDR) in Mbeo ;
3- Computerised cost price management in a furniture marketing company.
4- Functional study of a database of quotations from a public Higher Education and University establishment
5- Management and production of the customer database.

These are at least illustrative models for formulating subjects in business computing.

3- Data collection

The management computer exercises all the procedures detailed in the scientific research course, no other means of data collection, all the tools have been well defined in that course, and importantly, each field has its own particularities as outlined above.

To this end, the researcher must understand that:

- when the harvest is made, it is necessary to put in head that, those which receives it, do not have the only occupation although they have time for him, thus the saving of time of its share would be an element is not to forget, the researcher will have to have:

- simplicity in his style of language, his behaviour, his interview (interrogation) not complicating himself in vain ;
- the work he does has a timing, a minimum of wisdom to get it right.

For other points relating to research or data collection, especially in business computing, please refer to the Computer Analysis Method I course, "M.A.I1" in 2ème .

4- Work plan

It is a very important tool, channelling all the stages of the work, and comes from the Director/Framer,

As the person concerned is a neophyte, he needs a framer who will work under his auspices.

For us, in IT, the plan depends on and differs from one[6] cycle to another, and also takes into

[6] Diesta-Mputu, Notes de cours de Méthode d'analyse informatique II, G3/ Info INIGE, Kinshasa 2015

account the IT analysis method to be used.

While the scientific research course is concerned with general guidelines, the computer analysis method I, G2 course is very specific about how research should be carried out in this field. It supports the interview technique, which is the key to successful work in computer science, and can be carried out either face-to-face with the interviewees/users or using a pre-established questionnaire distributed to the interviewees.

Further on, emphasis is placed on ethics in general and in particular: behaviour, style, language, dress, etc. These elements are to be taken into account in their leaders. You have to know how to behave when you're working with them.

We have already said that no notion relating to the writing of a scientific paper should be left out. To this end, it is well known that the introduction (which may consist of the presentation of the subject, which is the general understanding of the subject to be dealt with, so that the reader has a brief overview) and the conclusion (which is the synthesis of the subject developed, which embodies the idea of each main line, it intensifies depending on the field) can never be lacking, knowing full well that the value of this work depends on the respect of all the assets.

1 - References

The research carried out: the reading, consultation of this or that book and other articles ... must be indicated at the bottom of the pages, see the scientific research course. This scientific honesty adds value to the work and specifies that the researcher has drawn on the skills of others.

The author has a free choice of terms and conditions, and there are at least three of them:

1- the references can go from the first page to the last, i.e. number them from 1 to the end of the work;

2- number them by section: partly according to the work structure ;

3- number them by page: each page must have its own references.

2- Bibliography

It is a directory of all the works consulted and read during the writing process; it must be made up of books, articles and works (TFC, Dissertation, Thesis, etc.) and a webography (websites consulted).

The bibliography must always be in order:

The order is based on authors' names (alphabetical order) or years of publication (ascending or descending order of years of publication).

3- Table of contents

As the name suggests, a table of contents lists at least the essential parts or important pages and adds their numbers.

N.B.: It should be noted that not every page can appear in the table of contents, as this does not encourage readers to make use of the work.

CHAPTER 2: RESPONSIBILITIES IN WRITING A SCIENTIFIC PAPER

In this section, we want to draw the researcher's attention (to the students of this decade). In MAI1, we said that the failure or success of a scientific work depends on the ability of the author himself. This may be due to his behaviour, his negligence, his incompetence or his irresponsibility.

Responsibility is a commitment that shows maturity and intelligence, to stand up for yourself, to do something in front of people, to demonstrate how you act and ...

The researcher/student must remember that he or she is the first person responsible for his or her scientific work, who will judge him or her, who will give him or her a decent job and who will award him or her a qualification for the rest of his or her life.

He has to be totally committed, understand what

he is doing and what he will do to show that he is the first author of his work.

He is the driving force, never letting up, but facing up to any eventuality. It's important to emphasise that if he fails, he's responsible, not someone else, which is why he's sent out into the field to investigate, to experience reality, to be one of the users. It is he who chose the subject and the field of investigation; failure is his own responsibility without prejudice.

Throughout the writing process, he had mastered the content of his subject, and the various discussions with his director/ supervisor had deepened his knowledge. How could he fail?

This is the fundamental reason for its responsibility for the result to be achieved.

2- Director/supervisor

Writing a scientific paper is always done under the eye of an experienced supervisor, who is the first advisor and guide not to be avoided.

a- Choosing the director/supervisor[7]

The choice of director/supervisor is free, in accordance with the same instructions issued by the Ministry of Education.

The student has the right to veto the appointment of

[7] Instruction 022 of the Higher Education and University of 2019.

any teacher as his or her supervisor, provided that the teacher is in the same field and works in the same institution as the student.

This overwhelming and voluntary freedom of choice for the framer activates him so that he is at ease in everything that is about to be undertaken.

b- Role of the director/supervisor

As we said earlier, it is the point of reference for any grey areas or difficulties that the student may encounter during the writing process.

The director is there to :

- Get him back on track;
- Drawing up the plan ;
- Help him to formulate the subject;
- Correcting him and finally, he is a close collaborator at all times.

Despite the fact that the researcher/student has been alone in the field/field of investigation, the contribution of his/her supervisor has an influence on the writing from start to finish; close collaboration with him/her is compulsory and should never be avoided. Just :

- This is the person who has the final say on the work deposit,
- before the defence, he has to coordinate everything,

- he has the backing of the defence;
- During the defence, he also has a say, in front of the members of the jury, and in the jury's deliberations.

It should be noted that the director may never write the assignment for his or her candidate. Strictly forbidden.

CHAPTER 3: THE STAGES OF SCIENTIFIC WORK IN BUSINESS INFORMATICS.

Computer science, being an exact science, has its own rigorous principles, and compliance with these will ensure total success. Non-compliance means failure, as Aristotle said, the principles of the excluded third[8] .

For us here, this editing goes from one cycle to another, because our computer analysis methods are required in relation to this cycle[9] .

In the first cycle, the recommended method is the method of computer analysis II "M.A.I 2", Merise advocates for all the steps allowed to get the real result, while in the second cycle, the three methods that are recommended, whose choice is relative to the interested party, are ;

- the IT project management method ;

---

[8] Principes et Sciences, Revues SN, Brussels, 2008.
[9] National Curriculum (PADM), IT course Page 299.

- IT audit
- and UML.

Despite the differences in computer analysis methods, they should follow the steps below:

Stage I: Opportunity study/preliminary analysis

This analysis of the existing situation undertakes to :

- present the field of investigation,
- its operation and organisation,
- its shortcomings (criticism of the existing system) and proposals to remedy the shortcomings identified.

At this stage, the researcher has not changed anything, except that he has to take the place of a user, so that he has in-depth knowledge of the old system, especially the key points. Then comes the criticism and the proposal of solutions to guide the future of the system.

Stage II: Designing the new system

While the first step was to gain an in-depth understanding of the field of investigation, the second is to highlight the solution adopted, taking into account all the shortcomings identified, in order to respond appropriately to the needs of the new system. And all computerised techniques must be applied.

From there, the IT solution will be taken into account in relation to its demonstrated advantages, so that this new system meets the requirements.

Stage III: Implementation

After the design stage comes the implementation of all the standards set in motion to ensure that the result can be experienced.

However, each stage can be broken down into different chapters, sections . . . depending on the type of subjects chosen, some of which are simple and others complex.

This is why we say that the number of pages in a scientific work in computer science has never been determined, because it varies as mentioned above. And any work that does not have all these four stages is botched, not worth the trouble. It must be rejected.

Stage IV: Programming

This final stage is the tangible result. Especially in the first cycle. Programming gives the final result, when the software has been well designed.

A FEW GUIDELINES TO FOLLOW

Process for preparing a scientific paper: dissertation/TFC

I - KEY ELEMENTS OF THE APPROACH

1- Work plan cfr. appendix

3- Written or oral questionnaire (see Annex)

II - CLARIFICATION OF SOME PARTS

a- Presentation of the subject

The presentation of the subject amounts to giving a general idea of the whole subject, which is comparable to the definition or defining a subject amounts to taking it word by word, but it would be better to paint a general picture.

b- Issues

Let's put it this way: the problematic is the hook, the central difficulty that torments the company, even though it already exists; the current approach consists of finding relief; this problematic is expressed by questions (±4) that we ask ourselves. They are deeply reflected in the subject explaining the major concern of the researcher, who must in turn undertake to find at least the ideal solution consoling the firm, it will be in the proposals made, demonstrating their rigidities. (See MRS)

c- Hypothesis

The hypothesis itself is a trial and error response to the problem, and this approach has not yet achieved its objective, nor have all the stages been completed to confirm the proposals adopted.

So all the questions reflecting the key ideal must at least be answered at this level, and these answers will directly guide the approach to be taken.

This must be demonstrated in the work, and every reader should be able to feel how the subject has been dressed up on these two points, which are on the one hand the major beam and on the other hand they make clear the mastery and knowledge of the subject.

III - RESEARCH QUESTIONNAIRE a-

Composition of the questionnaire (questions to be asked)

These questions provide the knowledge of what the end result should be. They are the basis for failure or success, and to achieve this, the technique must be applied properly, whether written or oral.

They originate in the mind of the researcher, while at the same time exploiting the subject within the overall objective and work plan.

b- Technique

The technique applauded is the "interview", because of the good results obtained by the pioneers in this field, and also because it offers good opportunities to ensure in-depth knowledge of the field being exploited.

Oral questions, i.e. being face-to-face with users, give us the opportunity to understand, to review, to correct, to recontact and even to ask questions where we haven't quite understood.

grabbed, that's how effective this interview technique is.

c- Key points of the interview

Three points can be highlighted in relation to our experience, which emphasises the advantage of the interview in facilitating the subject's approach.

1- understanding how things work

The researcher must ask questions about how the company operates, from its origins to its development:

a- general operations,

b- the different departments, their allocation, their tasks and their involvement in the operation of the system,

c- the different ways in which departments work together and the circulation of documents, all of which shape the flow of the system,

d- the different documents: their composition, their role, how they are filled in,

e- the different equipment used; the personnel: their qualifications, expertise, performance, seniority and function,

2- the difficulties they encounter in operating,

3- the solutions that users envisage for smooth operation in the future.

d- Conduct of the interview

1- Before the interview

Here we assume that you have been received and that you know the various departments with which you will be dealing, so you will need to inform the manager who will be receiving you, i.e. make an appointment to meet him or her on time.

a- have a good expression: politeness, gentleness, dress modestly,

b- behave in a manner befitting an academic.

2- During the interview

a- ask questions calmly and gently

b- let the other person speak

c- ask for time to take notes

3- After the interview

a- Go home and read the summary based on what you have understood; this gives you the opportunity to correct any omissions, etc.

b- knowing how to say thank you,

b- promise to return in the event of difficulties.

CHAPTER 4: WRITING THE ASSIGNMENT

Having been to the interview, and having understood what was done, the researcher is called upon to write up his work with the freshness of the knowledge acquired, while following the work plan and in the event of confusion, he can return to the field to his interlocutors or he can contact his director for the debates leading to the progress of the work.

SOME MODEL QUESTIONS TO ASK

I- History

1- When was your company founded?

2- What is its mission?

3- What is its geographical location?

II- How it works

1- What do you understand by .... (in the subject line)

2- How do you work?

3- What are the different documents that contribute to this process?

4- How important are they, how full are they, where do they come from?

III- Organisation

1- How are you organised?

2- What different departments contribute to this?

3- How do they work together?

3- What is the role of each of them?

IV- Resources

1- What type of staff do you have?

2- Their remit, function, grade, seniority, etc.

3- Their expertise?

3 - What equipment do you use? Their condition, use and year of purchase,

5- Where does your revenue come from?

6- Do you have a positive return?

7- Are you well looked after here?

V- Difficulties

1- What difficulties do you have, how do you

2- What solutions are you recommending?

2- What do you think of our visit here?

N.B.: There are no standard questions; they are relative to the subject and linked to the company's field or sector of activity.

The choice of Director is optional, and the candidate should consult an expert in the field for any shortcomings he or she may have.

In accordance with the instructions of the Ministry of Higher Education and Universities, the Director must be a member of the teaching staff of the same institution.

An illustration of the TFC Plan (undergraduate/graduate) :

INTRODUCTION

1- Presentation of the subject

2- Issues & Hypotheses

  1- Issues

  2- Assumptions

3- Choice & Interest of Subject

4- Methods and techniques used

1- Methods
2- Techniques
5- Limiting work
6- Difficulties encountered
6- Work outline

PART I: STUDY OF THE EXISTING SITUATION

CHAPTER I: KNOWLEDGE OF THE EXISTING SITUATION

I- Company presentation

1- Company history
2- Geographical location
3- Mission
1- Functional Structure
- Job descriptions

II - Study of the old System

1- General
2- Narration

a- Section I: Data

1- Documents directory
2- Description of documents

b- Section II: Treatments

1- General information on treatments
2- Flow chart
3- Departments involved in the study

c- Section: Resources

1- Human Resources
2- Material resources
3- Financial resources

CHAPTER II: CRITICISMS OF THE EXISTING

General points

1- Positive points

2- Negative points

3- Proposals & Suggestions

4- Choice of Solutions

1- Manual Solution

2- IT Solution 3 - Solution Adopted

PART II: DESIGNING THE NEW SYSTEM

CHAPTER III: CONCEPTUAL STAGE I - Conceptual Data Model

1- Drawing up the MCD

1- Basic concepts

2- Formalism

2- Management rules

3- Presentation of the MCD

- Inventory of objects and Relationships

II - Conceptual Processing Model (CPM)

1- Basic concepts

2- Formalism

CHAP. IV: ORGANISATIONAL STRUCTURE

I - MOD

1- Definition

2- MOD - MCD

3- Multiplication quantification

4- Quantifying properties

5- MOD volume calculation

6- Local MOD bypass

7- Data security

II - MOT

1- Goal

2- MCT - MOT

PART III: LOGICAL STEP

CHAPTER V: CREATION OF THE DATABASE

- General information

1- Origin of MLD

2- Relationship Diagram

3- Database volume: Indexes & Tables

4- Choice of IT equipment: DBMS & hardware

5- MLT

1- Basic concepts

2- Formalism

3- MOT - MLT

PART IV: IMPLEMENTATION OF THE DATABASE

CHAPTER VI: PHYSICAL DATA STAGE

1- Programming: Purpose

2- Choice of programming method

3- Tables presentation

4- Physical Data Model : Purpose

5- Application

Conclusion

Bibliography

Table of contents

OUTLINE OF THE MEMORY IN UML (cycle II/Licence) General Introduction 0- Presentation of the subject

1- Issues & Hypotheses

a- Issues

b- Hypothesis

2- Choice & Interest of Subject

a- Choice of subject

b-Interest in the subject

3- Work delimitation

4- Methods and techniques used

a- Methods

b- Techniques

5- Labour Subdivision

6- Difficulties encountered.

CHAPTER I: PRESENTATION OF THE FIELD OF INVESTIGATION

General

1- History

2- Geographical location of the field of investigation

3- Mission

4- Functional Structure

a- Organisational structure

b- Detailed study of workstations

CHAPTER II : STUDY OF THE EXISTING SYSTEM

General points

SECTION I: DATA

1- Documents directory

2- Description of documents

SECTION II: TREATMENTS

State of the question (narration)

1- The different Services

2- Structure concerned by the study

3- Flow chart

SECTION III: EXISTING RESOURCES General points

1- Human Resources

2- Material resources

3- Environmental Resources

4- Financial resources

CHAPTER III: CRITICISM OF THE EXISTING SYSTEM

General

1- Positive points

2- Negative points

3- Proposals and Suggested Solutions

---

a- Manual solution

b- IT solution

4- Choosing the Best Solution

CHAPTER IV : THE SYSTEM LEVEL STUDY

General points

1- Determining needs

a- Functional requirements

b- Non-functional needs

2- Detailed description of the project

1- Detailed study

a- Functional requirements

b- Non-functional accuracy

2- Identification of study stakeholders
3- Use Cases
a- Priority Use Cases
b- Secondary Use Cases
3- Presentation of Modelling Diagrams
4- Sequence diagram
5- Activity Diagram
6- Class diagram
a- Management rules
b- Class identification
c- Identifying relationships
d- Description
7- Presentation of the Class Diagram
8- Choice of IT equipment
Objectives

1- Software
2- Hardware
3- Staff

CHAPTER V: PLANNING THE STUDY
1- Time Evaluation
2- Resource Assessment
3- Cost evaluation
4- Gantt or Pert chart
General conclusion
Bibliography
Table of contents.

CONCLUSION

In conclusion, this booklet does not replace any research discipline; on the contrary, it provides a clear plan for computer scientists, first and foremost, to gather data effectively, in order to finally achieve the desired objective: "that of creating an appropriate computer system".

There may also be differences between other IT institutions, but what is useful is that the approach remains the same for all IT professionals.

All scientific disciplines use methods and techniques that enable them to achieve their objectives.

It's just one of a number of options. It's up to you to decide whether or not to use it.

All suggestions and comments are welcomed with open arms.

BIBLIOGRAPHY

1- Publications

1- Birou A., Vocabulaire pratique des Sciences Sociales, Editions ouvrières, Paris, 1966

2- Gordon Mace and Petry F. Guide d'élaboration d'un projet de recherches en Sciences Sociales, 3ed de Boeck, 2004

3- Shomba Kinyamba S., Méthodologie et Epistémologie de la recherche scientifique, PUK, Kinshasa, 2013.

4- Principes et Sciences, Revues SN, Brussels, 2008.

5- National Courses Programme (PADM), 2008

2- Other sources

1- Bokongo Libakea K. Notes de cours d'Initiation à la recherche scientifique, UPN, October 2005.

2- Diesta-Mputu, Notes de cours de Méthode d'analyse informatique II, G3/ Info INIGE, Kinshasa 2015

3- Diesta-Mputu, Information System Design (ISC) Course Notes, LVInfo ISC-Idiofa 2018

4- Diesta-Mputu, UML Notes, L2/Info ISC-Kikwit 2020

5- Instruction 022 de l'Enseignement Supérieur et Universitaire en RDCongo, 2019.

6- www.languefranqaise.uliege.be

7- Infotrack.unige

TABLE OF CONTENTS

Prelude 1
Introduction 4
GENERAL INFORMATION ON R WRITING A SCIENTIFIC PAPER. 6
1- Emergence of terms 9
2- The difference between intellectual work and scientific work. 10
CHAPTER 1: WRITING A SCIENTIFIC PAPER ON BUSINESS COMPUTING 19
CHAPTER 2: RESPONSIBILITIES IN WRITING A SCIENTIFIC PAPER 24
CHAPTER 3: THE STAGES OF SCIENTIFIC WORK IN BUSINESS INFORMATICS. 27
CHAPTER 4: DRAFTING THE WORK 33
SOME MODEL QUESTIONS TO ASK 34
CONCLUSION 42
BIBLIOGRAPHY 43
1- Works 43
2- Other sources 43
TABLE OF CONTENTS 44

MIX
Papier aus verantwortungsvollen Quellen
Paper from responsible sources
FSC® C105338

Printed by Books on Demand GmbH, Norderstedt / Germany